Editor

Mary S. Jones, M.A.

Editor in Chief

Karen J. Goldfluss, M.S. Ed.

Cover Artist

Barb Lorseyedi

Imaging

James Edward Grace

Craig Gunnell

Publisher

Mary D. Smith, M.S. Ed.

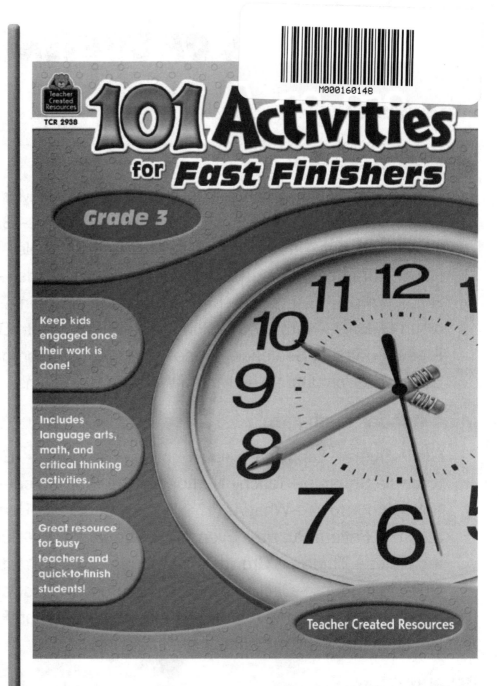

101 Activities for *Fast Finishers*

Grade 3

TCR 2938

Keep kids engaged once their work is done!

Includes language arts, math, and critical thinking activities.

Great resource for busy teachers and quick-to-finish students!

Teacher Created Resources

Teacher Created Resources

6421 Industry Way

Westminster, CA 92683

www.teachercreated.com

ISBN: 978-1-4206-2938-5

© 2011 Teacher Created Resources

Made in U.S.A.

Teacher Created Resources

TABLE OF CONTENTS

Introduction

All students work at different speeds. Many take about the same amount of time to finish their work. Some are slower than others, and some are faster than others. You've probably been asked, "I'm done, what do I do now?" more times than you can count. But what's a teacher to do when one or more students finish early? The activity pages in *101 Activities for Fast Finishers* are the answer.

The 101 activities in this book focus on language arts, math, and critical thinking, and are divided as follows:

- Lively Language Arts (35 activities)
- Mind-Bender Math (35 activities)
- Beyond Brainy (31 activities)

Each activity has been labeled with an approximate amount of time that it will take students to complete. The estimated times range from 5 to 15 minutes. It is recommended that you copy, in advance, several pages representing the different times, and have them on hand to distribute, as needed. When a student asks you that famous "What do I do now?" question, a quick look at the clock will tell you which activity to give him or her. These activities will also be helpful to keep in your emergency substitute file as filler activities.

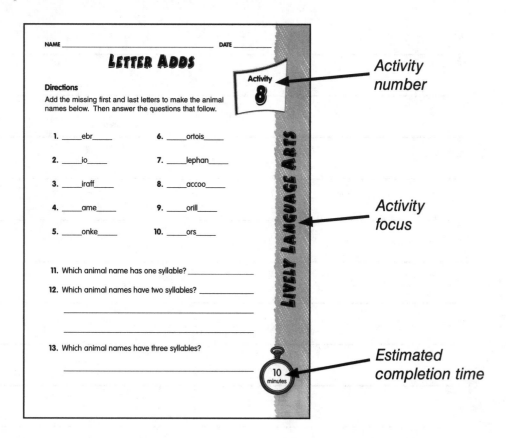

WORD MAKE

Activity 1

Directions

See how many words you can make by using the letters in the box. Each letter may be used only once in a word and no plurals are allowed.

m	t	a	e
c	p	l	s
k	i	b	n

_____ _____

_____ _____

_____ _____

_____ _____

_____ _____

_____ _____

_____ _____

LIVELY LANGUAGE ARTS

5 minutes

CONNECTIONS

Activity 2

Directions

Each word in the left box can be connected in some way with a word in the right box. Write the connecting word pairs on the lines.

down

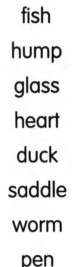

horse	fish
scales	hump
down	glass
paper	heart
camel	duck
bottle	saddle
silk	worm
kidney	pen

_____   _____
_____   _____
_____   _____
_____   _____
_____   _____
_____   _____
_____   _____

5 minutes

LIVELY LANGUAGE ARTS

FAST LIST

Activity **3**

Directions

Fill the spaces in the box with any letters you choose to make as many words as you can in five minutes. Write your LIST below.

LIVELY LANGUAGE ARTS

__ __ **S T**

_____ _____ _____

_____ _____ _____

_____ _____ _____

_____ _____ _____

_____ _____ _____

_____ _____ _____

_____ _____ _____

_____ _____ _____

_____ _____ _____

5 minutes

Be Words

Activity
4

Directions

All of the words below begin with "be." Write the full word that matches the meaning.

1. you sleep in it ⟶ be_____

2. an insect ⟶ be_____

3. it rings ⟶ be_____

4. hair on a man's face ⟶ be_____

5. a large animal ⟶ be_____

6. part of a bird ⟶ be_____

7. under ⟶ be_____

8. a small fruit ⟶ be_____

9. a vegetable ⟶ be_____

10. to start ⟶ be_____

LIVELY LANGUAGE ARTS

MIX AND MATCH

Activity
5

Directions

Mix and match the four word parts in each line to make two words.

Example: bo fi ok sh = book, fish

1.   ck   ft   so   du   _____

2.   nd   ld   ha   go   _____

3.   ri   ch   lo   ng   _____

4.   at   co   ng   so   _____

5.   aw   dr   re   ad   _____

6.   mo   fo   ot   on   _____

7.   op   wo   st   ol   _____

8.   wi   st   we   ng   _____

9.   ba   fe   et   ll   _____

10. ck   ll   be   so   _____

LIVELY LANGUAGE ARTS

10
minutes

COMPOUND WORDS

Activity 6

Directions

Unscramble the words in parentheses and write them on the lines. Then match the words on the left to the words on the right to make compound words.

1. rain   _____ (bkoo)

2. moon   _____ (rbshu)

3. life   _____ (tcoa)

4. note   _____ (ishp)

5. cross   _____ (rgaph)

6. tooth   _____ (cmbo)

7. photo   _____ (obat)

8. class   _____ (ilght)

9. space   _____ (moro)

10. honey   _____ (rdoa)

LIVELY LANGUAGE ARTS

10 minutes

FRONTS AND BACKS

Activity 7

Directions

The letters in the chart are the "fronts" and "backs" of words. See how many words you can make in five minutes using the "fronts" and "backs" provided.

Fronts	Backs
thr	ough
en	ead
alth	oat
spr	ifty
b	emy
n	ain
r	ing

LIVELY LANGUAGE ARTS

5 minutes

LETTER ADDS

Activity

8

Directions

Add the missing first and last letters to make the animal names below. Then answer the questions that follow.

1. _____ebr_____

2. _____io_____

3. _____iraff_____

4. _____ame_____

5. _____onke_____

6. _____ortois_____

7. _____lephan_____

8. _____accoo_____

9. _____orill_____

10. _____ors_____

LIVELY LANGUAGE ARTS

11. Which animal name has one syllable? _____

12. Which animal names have two syllables? _____

_____

_____

13. Which animal names have three syllables?

_____

10 minutes

BACK TO FRONT

Activity 9

Directions

Each of these words has its first part written last. Can you write each one correctly?

Example: okbo = book

1. oonball = _____

2. owsparr = _____

3. ballfoot = _____

4. terwin = _____

5. owyell = _____

6. berrystraw = _____

7. ourfl = _____

8. eymon = _____

9. eesech = _____

10. gerfin = _____

11. ypon = _____

12. tordoc = _____

13. lejung = _____

14. airch = _____

15. daybirth = _____

16. lepeop = _____

17. anteleph = _____

18. lestab = _____

5 minutes

PARTNER WORDS

Activity 10

Directions

Write the partner word for each given word on the line. Find each word in the grid and shade it in. Use a different color for each word. The first one is done for you.

1. pasta and _____sauce_____   5. bread and _____

2. bride and _____   6. salt and _____

3. fish and _____   7. knife and _____

4. bat and _____   8. ups and _____

c	h	i	p	s	p
b	j	a	m	d	e
a	g	s	f	o	p
l	r	a	o	w	p
l	o	u	r	n	e
x	o	c	k	s	r
q	m	e	t	z	u

LIVELY LANGUAGE ARTS

10 minutes

PICTURE THIS

Directions

Look at this picture of Brigit the Bricklayer.
Write down the names of all the things
in the picture that begin with the letter "b."

LIVELY LANGUAGE ARTS

_____

_____

_____

_____

10
minutes

Silent Letters

Directions

Read each word and choose the consonant that is silent. Write the letter in the box. Then write other words with silent letters as indicated below.

1. know ☐   **5.** half ☐

2. sign ☐   **6.** sword ☐

3. thumb ☐   **7.** write ☐

4. listen ☐   **8.** island ☐

9. silent w: _____

10. silent k: _____

11. silent b: _____

12. silent l: _____

LIVELY LANGUAGE ARTS

10 minutes

MISSING VOWELS

Directions

Add the missing vowels to complete each of these words. Use the clues in parentheses to help you.

1. f l ____ m ____ n g ____ → (bird)

2. s c h ____ ____ l → (place of learning)

3. t ____ n n ____ s → (sport)

4. q ____ ____ s t ____ ____ n → (opposite of answer)

5. t r ____ c t ____ r → (farm machine)

6. ____ c t ____ g ____ n → (shape)

7. n ____ w s p ____ p ____ r → (something to be read)

8. m ____ ____ n t ____ ____ n → (large hill)

9. p ____ n g ____ ____ n → (bird)

10. l ____ z ____ r d → (reptile)

11. l ____ t t ____ c ____ → (green vegetable)

12. l ____ b r ____ r y → (place for books)

5
minutes

16

LIVELY LANGUAGE ARTS

WORD CLOCK

Activity
14

Directions

Use the word clock to make as many words as you can in five minutes. One has been done for you.

b   m   h   s

j   tr

ch   str

ea

d   dr

cr   t

n

l   k   r   p

_____

_____

_____

_____

_____

heat

_____   _____   _____

_____   _____   _____

_____   _____   _____

_____   _____   _____

_____   _____   _____

_____   _____   _____

LIVELY LANGUAGE ARTS

5
minutes

LETTER ROWS

LIVELY LANGUAGE ARTS

Directions

Look at each row of letters in the chart, and then answer the questions below.

1	k	p	l	o	n	m	q
2	t	p	s	o	x	t	v
3	e	t	v	e	e	w	b
4	m	o	n	k	e	y	s
5	a	i	u	o	e	a	u
6	i	f	e	d	b	c	a

1. Which row has only vowels? _____

2. In which rows do all the letters come after "j" in the alphabet? _____

3. In which row does the same vowel appear three times?

   _____

4. Which row spells the name of some animals?

   _____

5. In which row do all the letters come before "j" in the alphabet? _____

6. Make five words using the first four letters in row 2.

   _____

10
minutes

CRAMPED WORDS

Directions

When this list of words was being typed, it became very cramped. Can you figure out what each word is? The clues below will help you. Write each word beside its clue.

mouseduckfoursickpinklionfirstcitydrysnakeshoespony

1. not well   _____

2. large cat   _____

3. reptile   _____

4. number   _____

5. small horse   _____

6. opposite of last   _____

7. large town   _____

8. not wet   _____

9. color   _____

10. bird   _____

11. footwear   _____

12. small creature   _____

10
minutes

LIVELY LANGUAGE ARTS

SYNONYMS

Directions

Draw lines matching the synonyms in columns
A, B, and C. One has been done for you.

LIVELY LANGUAGE ARTS

Column A	Column B	Column C
able	capable	ask
alarm	error	blunder
big	frighten	competent
danger	globe	Earth
divide	huge	hazard
hurt	injure	large
interrogate	peril	split
mistake	question	terrify
world	separate	wound

10 minutes

HIDDEN WORDS

Activity 18

Directions

Write down the first letter of these scrambled words, and then add every second letter. You will find the names of different things to eat. Then write these foods in alphabetical order in the box below.

LIVELY LANGUAGE ARTS

1. hxatmpbzusrtgxesr

_____

2. pxetayczh

_____

3. btaznxaxnpa

_____

4. ayvpozcxaydfo

_____

5. cthpexexsye

_____

6. cxutcduxmpbxetr

_____

7. ltexmyopn

_____

8. atpzrfixcyott

_____

Alphabetical Order

a. _____   e. _____

b. _____   f. _____

c. _____   g. _____

d. _____   h. _____

10 minutes

MULTIPLE MEANINGS

LIVELY LANGUAGE ARTS

Activity 19

Directions

Color the correct word in the box that matches the word or phrase on the left.

1.	story	tale		tail
2.	rabbit	hare		hair
3.	bus token	fair		fare
4.	odor	sent		scent
5.	make a purchase	buy	by	bye
6.	one	lone		loan
7.	also	to	two	too
8.	assistant	aid		aide
9.	land by a lake	beach		beech
10.	two	pear		pair
11.	large	great		grate
12.	change	alter		altar
13.	atmosphere	air		heir
14.	grief	mourning		morning
15.	land	aisle		isle

10 minutes

SMALL WORDS

Activity 20

Directions

Use the small words from the box to complete the names of these animals

bit	row	sum	key	can
rot	pen	edge	or	at
her	bra	all	top	

1. p l ___ ___ y p u s

2. h ___ ___ ___ ___ h o g

3. ___ ___ ___ g u i n

4. m o n ___ ___ ___

5. s p a r ___ ___ ___

6. ___ ___ ___ i g a t o r

7. z e ___ ___ ___

6. o p o s ___ ___ ___

7. r a b ___ ___ ___

8. s t ___ ___ k

9. p a r ___ ___ ___

10. p e l i ___ ___ ___

13. o c ___ ___ ___ u s

14. p a n t ___ ___ ___

5 minutes

"EA" WORDS

Activity
21

Directions

All of the words in the box are "ea" words. Think about the sounds made by the vowel pair "ea." Sort the words based on their vowel sounds. Write the words on the correct loaf of bread.

steak	scream	seats	already
heavy	deaf	weather	reading
treat	bread	steal	breath
measure	wealth	ahead	speak
bead	meant	great	instead
death	repeat	leaf	break

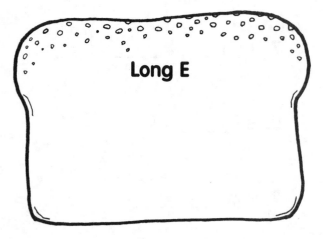

Long E

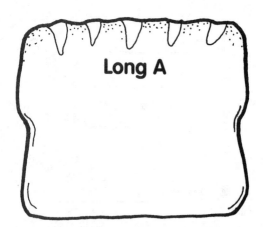

Long A

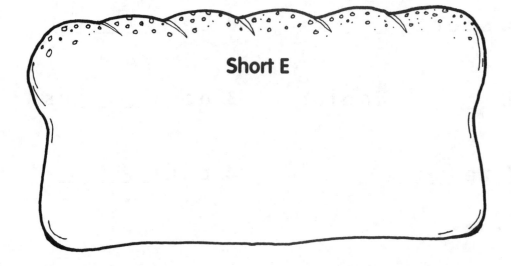

Short E

10
minutes

COMMON LETTERS

Activity
22

Directions

In the words *must*, *thrash*, *team*, *pester*, and *steam*, the only letter that appears in every word is "t." Write down the letter that appears in each of the words in the following groups.

					Common Letter
1. coast	roast	must	team	store	
2. pair	pear	ripe	peer	rare	
3. union	gruel	purse	pull	ruthless	
4. easily	trees	easel	Easter	pea	
5. dawn	wheel	wealth	drawn	prawn	
6. smooth	mouth	might	mostly	moon	

5 minutes

LIVELY LANGUAGE ARTS

SORTING

Directions

Place the words in the box in their correct tree below.

beige	lettuce	lizard	yellow
cabbage	penguin	violet	squash
ostrich	crocodile	turnip	swallow
gecko	purple	sparrow	snake

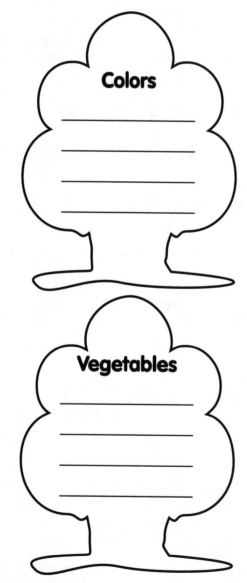

Colors

Birds

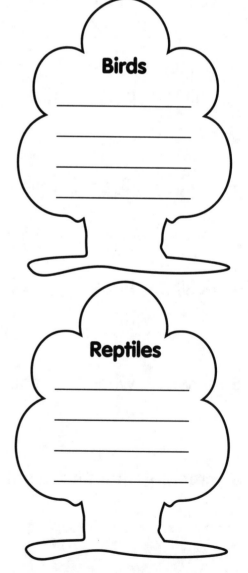

Vegetables

Reptiles

LIVELY LANGUAGE ARTS

5 minutes

SPECIAL PLURALS

Activity 24

Directions

Some plural names are unusual. Write the unusual plural for each noun below. Then find the unusual plurals in the word search.

1. goose _____

2. mouse _____

3. foot _____

4. man _____

5. person _____

6. child _____

7. woman _____

8. ax _____

g	e	e	s	e	n	e	m
f	n	e	m	o	w	l	d
p	x	w	m	i	a	p	g
a	k	j	v	z	c	o	t
c	h	i	l	d	r	e	n
n	p	e	t	h	e	p	b
d	a	u	p	f	o	e	y

LIVELY LANGUAGE ARTS

15 minutes

NOUN RIDDLES

Activity
25

Directions

Nouns are the names of things all around us. See if you can solve the riddles below. Write the noun on the line.

1. I have hooves.
   I run fast.
   I have a mane.
   I am a _____.

2. I hatch from an egg.
   I have sharp teeth.
   I am long and green.
   I like water.
   I am a _____.

3. I have a horn.
   I can go fast or slow.
   I take people places.
   I have seatbelts.
   I am a _____.

4. I am small.
   I can fly.
   I can be annoying.
   I can carry germs.
   I am a _____.

5. I am in the country.
   Some animals live on me.
   I have a barn and a yard.
   I am a _____.

6. I am sneaky.
   I am orange and black.
   I have stripes.
   I can run very fast.
   I am a _____.

7. I am green.
   There are lights all over me.
   Gifts are placed beneath me.
   I am a _____.

8. I am white.
   I am served cold.
   I go well with cereal.
   I come from an animal.
   I am _____.

9. I am big.
   I love garbage.
   I drive around town.
   I pick up trash cans.
   I am a _____.

10. I am sometimes called grand.
    I have keys on me.
    I am usually black and white.
    I make pretty music.
    I am a _____.

11. I am bright.
    I am made of gas.
    I am high in the sky.
    I am a _____.

12. I am soft.
    People sit on me.
    I have cushions.
    I am a _____.

LIVELY LANGUAGE ARTS

10 minutes

VERBALLY SPEAKING

Directions

"Saying verbs" express spoken actions. Add a "saying verb" from the box to complete each sentence below.

hooted	screaming	tell	yelled	whispered
shouted	said	hissed	talk	barking

1. The boy _____ the answer to his neighbor.

2. The fans were _____ as the team ran onto the field.

3. The audience _____ as the villain took to the stage.

4. My mom _____ that three friends could spend the night.

5. The substitute will _____ the teacher everything we do.

6. Last night, the neighbor's dog was _____.

7. The boy _____ as loud as he could.

8. The girls _____ when they saw the mask.

9. They _____ on the phone at least twice a day!

10. The owl _____ across the trees.

LIVELY LANGUAGE ARTS

10 minutes

GUIDE WORDS

Activity
27

Directions

To look up words in the dictionary, you need to know guide words. Guide words are the two words at the top of the page. The word on the left tells you the beginning word on the page, and the word on the right tells you the last word on the page.

Put a checkmark (✓) next to the words you would find on each of these dictionary pages.

LIVELY LANGUAGE ARTS

barrel	cabin

1.
_____ beast
_____ bar
_____ belt
_____ canoe

lumber	mayor

2.
_____ load
_____ march
_____ melt
_____ laid
_____ lump

Now put a checkmark (✓) next to the words you would **not** find on the page.

smooth	thick

3.
_____ tap
_____ thief
_____ smoke
_____ ship
_____ team

10 minutes

IN ORDER

Activity
28

Directions

Put these lists of events into chronological order by numbering them from first (1) to last (5).

1. _____ eat breakfast

_____ wake up

_____ go to school

_____ go out the door

_____ brush teeth

2. _____ bait a hook

_____ clean a fish

_____ eat a fish

_____ catch a fish

_____ cook a fish

3. _____ mail the letter

_____ put the letter in an envelope

_____ write the letter

_____ wait for an answer

_____ seal the envelope

4. _____ write book report

_____ type book report

_____ turn on printer

_____ turn on computer

_____ print book report

5. _____ slap my arm

_____ see a mosquito

_____ feel a bite

_____ hear a buzz

_____ scratch a bump

6. _____ buy popcorn

_____ leave the theater

_____ stand in line

_____ buy a ticket

_____ watch a movie

LIVELY LANGUAGE ARTS

10 minutes

Sequencing Events

Activity 29

Directions

Read the story. Then write the events below in story order.

On the night before her family vacation, Tracy began packing. She needed clothes that would keep her warm in the mountains. Tracy packed a coat and many warm sweaters. Then she packed some long pants, socks, and boots. Finally, Tracy packed some cozy pajamas. Just as she was ready to close her suitcase, she remembered her journal. She wanted to write about every detail of her vacation. As Tracy lay on her bed thinking of her exciting trip, she drifted off to sleep.

1. _____

2. _____

3. _____

4. _____

5. _____

- Tracy packed her socks.
- Tracy fell asleep.
- Tracy packed her pajamas.
- Tracy packed her journal.
- Tracy packed her coat.

10 minutes

MAKING SENTENCE SENSE

Activity
30

Directions

Pick the word from the box that completes each sentence. Write it on the line with a capital letter. Cross out the word after you have used it. Add a punctuation mark at the end of the sentence.

look	get	wow	clean	how	did	let	please
why	she	stop	were	those	they	what	~~where~~

Example: __Where__ did you find his backpack ?

1. _____ go of that ☐

2. _____ worked together to search through the boxes ☐

3. _____ would anyone steal an old stamp album ☐

4. _____ lifted the treasure chest's lid and peeked inside ☐

5. _____ away from those flames ☐

6. _____ the bus at the fourth house on the left ☐

7. _____ Uncle Scott say "yes" or "no" ☐

8. _____ answer the question ☐

9. _____ the fawns near our trailer ☐

10. _____, that's awful ☐

11. _____ are my shoes ☐

12. _____ out below ☐

13. _____ the shower stall ☐

14. _____ much does this video game system cost ☐

15. _____ is wrong with the microwave ☐

10
minutes

LIVELY LANGUAGE ARTS

PAST TENSE

Activity
31

Directions

The words below are in the present tense.
Write them in the past tense on the lines, and
then find them in the word search.

```
U  M  D  U  R  D  E  T  F  S  C  T  T
N  B  W  E  N  I  H  E  U  D  O  O  T
D  O  R  U  D  R  Z  R  F  W  O  F  U
E  U  O  E  E  I  P  W  E  T  K  M  V
R  F  K  W  C  R  C  N  D  S  E  T  Q
S  G  W  P  I  O  K  E  J  X  D  U  P
T  H  N  S  T  B  G  D  D  D  R  A  N
O  B  E  A  D  E  D  N  E  T  E  R  P
O  D  U  K  S  U  C  I  I  K  R  N  A
D  G  S  L  L  T  L  A  D  Z  S  G  V
H  C  L  A  P  P  E  D  U  R  E  A  N
E  V  U  Y  E  D  P  D  H  G  O  D  A
M  J  J  R  T  O  G  R  O  F  H  V  G
A  L  E  F  T  R  O  E  M  A  C  T  E
```

ASK _____   DRIVE _____   RECOGNIZE _____

CATCH _____   FIND _____   REPLY _____

CLAP _____   FORGET _____   SING _____

COME _____   KNOW _____   SURPRISE _____

COOK _____   LEAVE _____   THROW _____

DECIDE _____   PRETEND _____   UNDERSTAND _____

15 minutes

COMPARING OBJECTS

Directions

Read each sentence. Compare the objects by using the correct form of the descriptive words in the box. Write your answers on the lines. One has been done for you.

tall	cold	loud	warm	heavy
fast	tiny	messy	soft	bright

1. Her blanket is _____**softer**_____ than mine.

2. The Empire State Building is _____ than my house.

3. August is usually the _____ month of the year.

4. A cheetah is the _____ land animal.

5. After painting in class, Tim's clothes were the _____.

6. The brick is _____ than the feather.

7. The kitchen light is the _____ one in the house.

8. A ladybug is _____ than a butterfly.

9. The emergency siren is the _____ noise I've ever heard.

10. It is _____ in the mountains than at the beach.

SENTENCE WORD ORDER

**Activity
33**

Directions

Read each set of words. Put the words in order to form a sentence. Write it on the line. When you see (ask), make the sentence into a question.

Example: stay should after I today and Bryan school (ask)

Should Bryan and I stay after school today?

1. your white have grandma hair does (ask)

_____

2. found Jacki wallet a yesterday

_____

3. just star saw shooting a I

_____

4. hide you the money did (ask)

_____

5. this won he race afternoon the

_____

6. game ask you will for a (ask)

_____

7. chasing puppy stop the

_____

8. find my homework missing Victoria did (ask)

_____

9. working refrigerator my stopped has

_____

10. quickly the crossed Logan over bridge

_____

LIVELY LANGUAGE ARTS

15 minutes

RHYMING WORD PAIRS

Directions

Find two words that rhyme together and have about the same meaning as the phrase that is given. An example has been done for you.

bashful insect = shy fly

1. chicken yard _____

2. distant sun _____

3. warm pan _____

4. rabbit stool _____

5. boat journey _____

6. untied bird _____

7. good nap _____

8. angry father _____

9. large fake hair _____

10. reading area _____

11. not fast bird _____

12. a group of noon eaters _____

13. damp plane _____

14. kind rodents _____

15. kitty cap _____

LIVELY LANGUAGE ARTS

15 minutes

IDIOMS

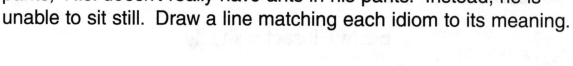

Activity 35

Directions

Idioms are phrases that have special meanings. For example, in the phrase "R.J. has ants in his pants," R.J. doesn't really have ants in his pants. Instead, he is unable to sit still. Draw a line matching each idiom to its meaning.

1. Carmella is all ears.   acting or looking the same

2. "Hold your horses!" said the police officer.   teasing

3. Ava is getting hot under the collar.   needs to hurry

4. "Quit pulling my leg!" said Mr. Zen.   getting angry

5. "Doesn't this story ring a bell?" asked Ken.   ready to go

6. Justin is always on the ball.   slow down

7. Don needs to get to class on the double.   in good shape

8. Gordon is skating on thin ice.   remind you of something

9. Abigail and Ali are like two peas in a pod!   getting into trouble

10. Grandma likes to keep herself fit as a fiddle.   listening carefully

10 minutes

CIRCLE SUMS

Activity 36

Directions

Color the two numbers in each wheel that add up to the number in its center. Can you finish in under five minutes?

1.

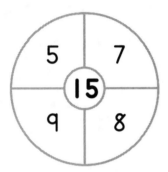

2.

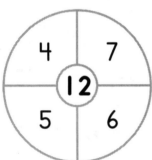

3.

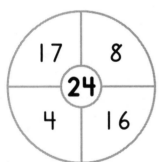

4.

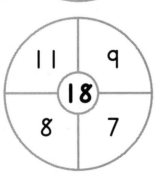

5.

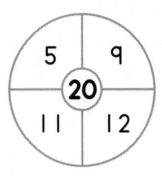

6.

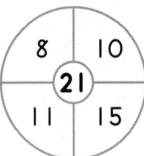

7.

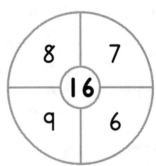

8.

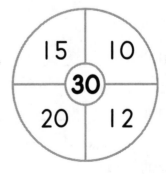

5 minutes

MIND-BENDER MATH

ZAPPING

Directions

Tony zapped four spaceships on his video game. His total score was 25. Write the different combinations of spaceships that he could have zapped.

MIND-BENDER MATH

Combination 1 : _____

Combination 2 : _____

10 minutes

Combination 3 : _____

40

SKIP COUNTING

Directions

Count by 3s to 60 and color the path red.

Count by 4s to 60 and color the path blue.

4s path   3s path

7	9	11	4	3	9	12	7	3	9	18	11	14
12	13	14	6	8	12	8	6	63	6	17	21	20
8	3	7	5	9	16	5	4	36	16	9	19	18
5	11	8	7	6	20	3	2	81	17	11	12	3
60	4	32	28	24	33	2	1	64	18	15	16	1
56	3	36	9	16	94	30	27	24	21	53	61	60
52	12	40	54	18	68	33	10	7	45	48	97	57
62	48	44	71	51	13	36	39	42	61	65	51	54

MIND-BENDER MATH

5 minutes

FOURTEENS

Activity
39

Directions

Color all the number pairs that are connected at a side and add up to 14. One has been done for you. Color each pair a different color.

8	7	7	10	5	9
6	4	2	1	13	3
11	3	8	6	2	11
9	5	1	7	4	5
6	8	12	2	10	9

MIND-BENDER MATH

10 minutes

EQUAL SUMS

Directions

Fill in the missing digits in the shapes below. The sum of the three digits in each straight line should be the same.

1.

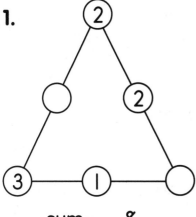

sum = __8__

4.

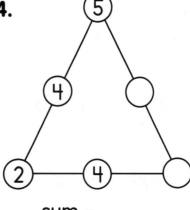

sum = _____

2.

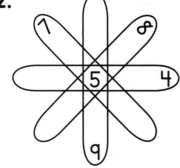

sum = __15__

5.

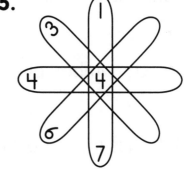

sum = __12__

3.

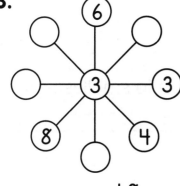

sum = __18__

6.

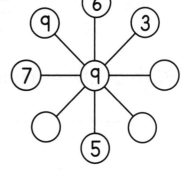

sum = _____

10 minutes

MIND-BENDER MATH

Number Knows

Activity
41

Directions

Look at the numbers carefully, and then answer the questions.

481	563	291	92	123	39	365

1. Which is the largest number in the box? _____

2. Which is the smallest number in the box? _____

3. Which is the only even number? _____

4. Which number, plus 9, would equal 300? _____

5. Which is the largest of the odd numbers? _____

6. Which two numbers consist of exactly the same digits but in a different order? _____

7. Write all of these numbers from largest to smallest.

_____

SQUARES

Activity
42

Directions

How many squares are there altogether in this shape?

There are _____ total squares.

TOUCHY NUMBERS

Activity
43

Directions

Fill in the blank boxes with the numbers 1–5. Each full row and column contains the numbers 1, 2, 3, 4, and 5. Each shaded number is the sum of all the numbers touching it.

1.

	2		1	
1	23	2	23	3
2	5		4	
4	27	4	24	5
	3	1	4	

2.

5		3	1	
4	33	5	21	3
3	5		2	
1	21	2	24	5
2		1		4

10
minutes

MIND·BENDER MATH

COUNT THE DICE

Directions

Count the dots on the dice. Record the number and the written form. The first one has been done for you.

MIND-BENDER MATH

Dice	Number	Written Form
1.	341	three hundred forty-one
2.		
3.		
4.		
5.		
6.		
7.		
8.		

10 minutes

OPERATION BOXES

Activity
45

Directions

Fill in each blank box with a number so that everything that touches is true and positive.

1.

+		=		
3		1	−	
=	7			=
	−			2
		=	3	+

Start →

2.

−		=	9	=
		7		
=		+		+
1		2 ↑		4

Start

5 minutes

FOLLOWING ARROWS

Activity
46

Directions

In each column, start with the number given, and then follow the instructions until you reach the bottom of the column. Circle your final number.

1. Start with 3	2. Start with 10	3. Start with 8
↓	↓	↓
double it = _____	halve it = _____	double it = _____
↓	↓	↓
add 4 = _____	multiply by 3 = ____	add 20 = _____
↓	↓	↓
double it = _____	double it = _____	subtract 5 = _____
↓	↓	↓
add 10 = _____	add 20 = _____	double it = _____
↓	↓	↓
take away 5 = _____	add 30 = _____	add 8 = _____
↓	↓	↓
add 15 = _____	add 20 = _____	double it = _____

MIND-BENDER MATH

5 minutes

WHAT AM I?

Activity

47

Directions

Solve the number riddles below.

1. I am odd.

I am less than 10.

I am the largest single digit you can write.

I am

2. I am even and I am less than 10.

I am more than a pair.

You can count me on one hand.

I am

3. I am a number between 10 and 20.

I am odd.

The sum of my digits is 8.

I am

4. I am more than 10 but less than 20.

I am even.

The sum of my digits is 9.

I am

5. I am an even number between 20 and 30.

I am divisible by 2, 4, 6, and 12.

The sum of my digits is 6.

I am

MIND-BENDER MATH

5
minutes

PATTERN SQUARES

Activity
48

Directions

Look at the number pattern in each square. One number is missing. Write the missing number in each square.

1.

1	2	3
4	5	
7	8	9

4.

1	6	11
16		26
31	36	41

2.

28	32	36
40	44	
52	56	60

5.

3		9
12	15	18
21	24	27

3.

2	4	6
8	10	12
	16	18

6.

2	4	8
16		64
128	256	512

MIND-BENDER MATH

5
minutes

BEAN BAG TOSS

Activity
49

Directions

Solve each word problem. The bean bag can hit the same number more than once.

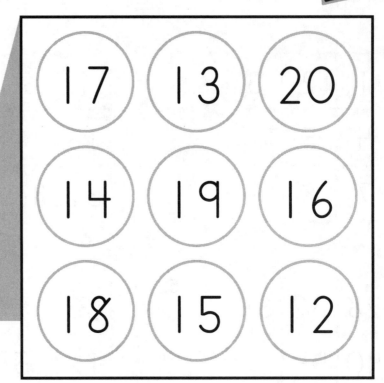

MIND-BENDER MATH

5 minutes

1. Thomas threw two bean bags. The difference between the numbers is 3. The smaller number is larger than 16. What two numbers did Thomas hit?

_____ and _____

2. Bill threw two bean bags. The difference between the numbers is 1. Both numbers are less than 14. What are the two numbers?

_____ and _____

3. Jan threw two bean bags. The difference between the numbers is 5. The larger number is 17. What is the smaller number?

_____

4. Wilma threw two bean bags. The difference between the numbers is 4. One of the numbers is 17. What is the other number?

_____

How Much?

Directions

Solve each subtraction problem. Use your answers to solve the riddle below by matching each letter to its answer.

1. $84.67
  – $44.12
  (R)

2. $88.02
  – $70.01
  (G)

3. $14.07
  – $12.07
  (O)

4. $97.11
  – $17.11
  (W)

5. $91.60
  – $90.12
  (S)

6. $22.18
  – $10.09
  (O)

7. $67.07
  – $23.68
  (G)

8. $21.22
  – $15.02
  (E)

9. $76.43
  – $16.23
  (E)

10. $19.19
  – $12.07
  (I)

11. $33.87
  – $12.22
  (R)

12. $87.66
  – $40.22
  (T)

13. $39.19
  – $30.09
  (N)

14. $55.55
  – $45.35
  (N)

MIND-BENDER MATH

Where will you never find money?

___ ___ ___ ___ ___ ___ ___
$43.39 $40.55 $2.00 $80.00 $7.12 $10.20 $18.01

___ ___ ___ ___ ___ ___ ___
$12.09 $9.10 $47.44 $21.65 $6.20 $60.20 $1.48

15
minutes

PATTERN PUZZLE

Directions

Find the pattern relating the first two rows of numbers in the table to the bottom row. Then complete each table and write the rule for each one.

1.

4	9	8	7	9	11	15	16	14	13	17	21	25
3	4	6	7	8	7	6	8	10	11	6	9	8
7	13											

Rule: _____

2.

2	4	5	6	7	5	8	5	9	7	8	10	6
3	2	3	3	4	4	3	5	5	2	5	10	4
6	8											

Rule: _____

3.

10	8	11	12	14	19	12	16	20	30	13	17	100
5	3	4	6	4	8	7	10	11	1	7	12	20
5	5											

Rule: _____

10 minutes

EVENS OUT

Activity
52

Directions

Cross out the letters in the boxes that have even numbers beside them. Use the leftover letters in each row to make a word that fits the definitions below.

1. 9 a	7 e	8 s	3 z	5 r	4 p	7 b
2. 9 l	17 e	21 a	13 p	8 m	7 p	12 n
3. 17 r	14 x	11 b	100 t	15 o	21 m	27 o
4. 9 n	21 e	20 t	40 m	25 r	65 g	73 e
5. 86 p	17 s	35 e	41 u	57 o	14 t	63 m
6. 72 m	7 r	19 t	99 t	85 e	37 u	25 b

MIND-BENDER MATH

Row 1: striped animal _____

Row 2: fruit _____

Row 3: for cleaning _____

Row 4: color _____

Row 5: small animal _____

Row 6: food from milk _____

5
minutes

EQUAL PARTS

MIND-BENDER MATH

Directions

Color or circle the shapes that have equal parts as indicated at the top of each box.

1. four equal parts

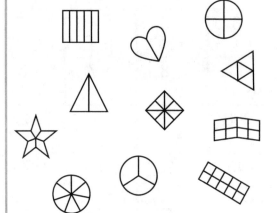

2. three equal parts

3. two equal parts

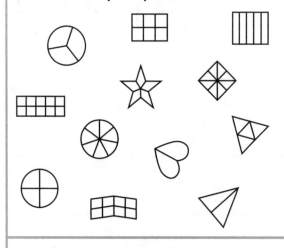

4. five equal parts

5. six equal parts

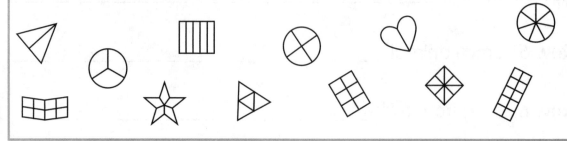

5 minutes

SQUARE TIMES

Activity
54

Directions

If each square equals three, what are the following shapes worth?

1. _____

4. _____

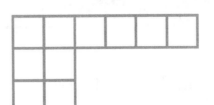

2. _____

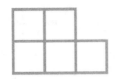

5. _____

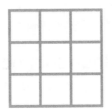

3. _____

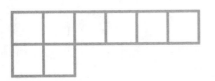

6. _____

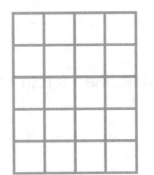

MIND-BENDER MATH

5 minutes

FOLLOW THE RULES

Activity

55

Directions

Complete the table by following each rule.

MIND-BENDER MATH

	Rule	18	40	6	32	10	24
1.	add 2; then double		84				
2.	subtract 5; then multiply by 2						
3.	triple; then subtract 5						
4.	add 2; then divide by 2						
5.	double; then subtract 10						

10 minutes

58

THREE'S A CROWD

Activity

56

Directions

Solve the multiplication facts for the number 3. Then find and color these number words in the grid. Use a different color for each one.

1. 3 x 1 = _____   **5.** 3 x 5 = _____   **9.** 3 x 9 = _____

2. 3 x 2 = _____   **6.** 3 x 6 = _____   **10.** 3 x 10 = _____

3. 3 x 3 = _____   **7.** 3 x 7 = _____   **11.** 3 x 11 = _____

4. 3 x 4 = _____   **8.** 3 x 8 = _____   **12.** 3 x 12 = _____

t	w	e	l	v	e	n	i	n	e	x	h	e
f	t	h	i	r	t	y	s	i	x	d	s	i
i	t	t	w	e	n	t	y	o	n	e	i	g
f	h	e	i	g	h	t	e	e	n	f	x	h
t	i	t	h	r	e	e	f	o	u	r	n	t
e	r	t	w	e	n	t	y	f	o	u	r	o
e	t	t	h	i	r	t	y	t	h	r	e	e
n	y	t	w	e	n	t	y	s	e	v	e	n

13. Can you find two numbers in the grid that are not part of the 3 x multiplication facts? Circle them.

10 minutes

MIND-BENDER MATH

FISHY TALES

MIND-BENDER MATH

Directions

Alex catches fish that have an **odd** number for their answer. Nina catches fish that have an <u>even</u> number for their answer. Color the fish using <u>blue</u> for <u>Nina</u> and **red** for **Alex** to show who catches which fish.

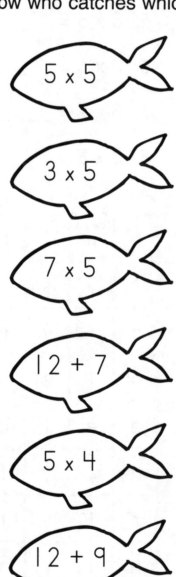

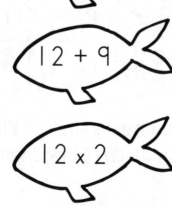

3 x 4   5 x 5   8 + 8

9 x 2   3 x 5   3 x 7

6 x 2   7 x 5   7 x 2

5 x 3   12 + 7   8 + 10

15 + 6   5 x 4   3 x 3

7 + 5   12 + 9   4 x 4

7 x 3   12 x 2

10 minutes

QUICK CALCULATIONS

Activity
58

Directions

Answer these as quickly as you can. See if you can get them all right in less than five minutes.

1. $8 + 3 + 4 =$ _____

2. $1/2$ of $20 =$ _____

3. $2 \times 5 =$ _____

4. $(7 \times 2) + 5 =$ _____

5. $20 - 2 - 2 =$ _____

6. $11 + 4 + 5 =$ _____

7. double $6 =$ _____

8. $(2 \times 4) + 7 =$ _____

9. $(5 \times 4) - 3 =$ _____

10. days in 2 weeks = _____

11. $10 \times$ _____ $= 100$

12. cents in $1.65 =$ _____

13. 8 more than $16 =$ _____

14. 7 less than $16 =$ _____

15. $40 - 4 - 4 =$ _____

16. $(2 \times 20) + 10 =$ _____

17. odd numbers between 10 and 20 = _____

_____

18. in digits: one hundred nine

_____

MIND-BENDER MATH

5 minutes

ALL TIED UP

MIND-BENDER MATH

Directions

Draw lines from each balloon to the right person's hand. Use a different color for each person's balloons.

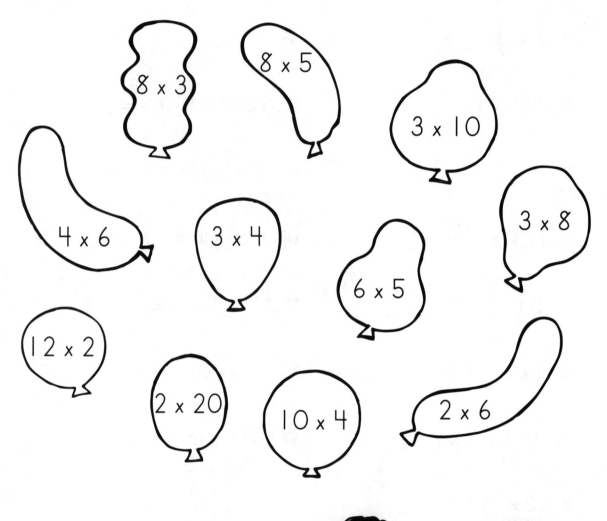

8 x 3

8 x 5

3 x 10

4 x 6

3 x 4

3 x 8

6 x 5

12 x 2

2 x 20

10 x 4

2 x 6

5 minutes

24

12

40

30

FRUIT LOOPS

Activity
60

Directions

Multiply the number above each box by 3. Use your answers and the Code Breaker to find the name of each fruit.

Code Breaker										
21	24	30	33	15	12	18	27	9	36	3
a	b	e	g	l	n	o	p	r	c	h

1. 9 10 7 3

☐ ☐ ☐ ☐

2. 7 9 9 5 10

☐ ☐ ☐ ☐ ☐

3. 9 10 7 12 1

☐ ☐ ☐ ☐ ☐

4. 8 7 4 7 4 7

☐ ☐ ☐ ☐ ☐ ☐

5. 6 3 7 4 11 10

☐ ☐ ☐ ☐ ☐ ☐

6. 11 3 7 9 10

☐ ☐ ☐ ☐ ☐

5
minutes

CIRCLING AROUND

Activity
61

Directions

Complete the number wheels by filling in the correct numbers on the outside of the circles.

1.

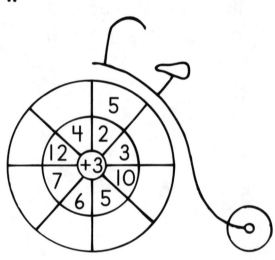

3.

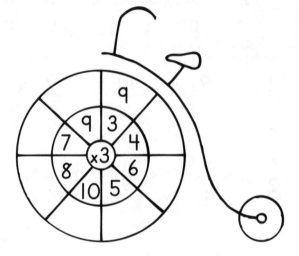

2.

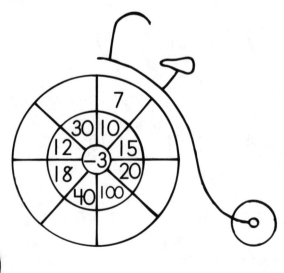

4.

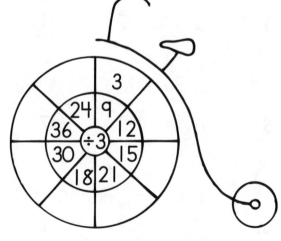

5 minutes

SUM IT UP

Directions

Solve the math problems, and then color the answers in the grid.

1	2	3	4	5	6
7	8	9	10	11	12
13	14	15	16	17	18
19	20	21	22	23	24
25	26	27	28	29	30
31	32	33	34	35	36

1. double 9 = _____ = yellow

2. half of 24 = _____ = red

3. 8 + 10 + 8 = _____ = pink

4. 40 – 5 = _____ = brown

5. (2 x 10) + 13 = _____ = green

6. (20 ÷ 2) + (15 ÷ 5) = _____ = blue

7. 2 x 4 x 3 = _____ = orange

8. 8 more than 17 = _____ = purple

ANSWER MATCH

Activity
63

Directions

Look at the left and right sides in the columns below. On each side, there are equations that have the same answer. Draw lines between equations that have the same answer. The first one has been done for you.

21 – 15	5 x 3
4 + 5	5 x 7
36 – 24	3 x 4
13 + 8	2 x 3
38 – 11	7 x 4
9 + 15	7 x 7
45 – 13	8 x 8
3 + 12	9 x 6
17 + 18	3 x 3
22 + 23	3 x 7
46 – 16	3 x 9
19 + 23	7 x 9
60 – 12	8 x 5
13 + 15	8 x 2
12 + 37	4 x 6
33 + 30	4 x 8
77 – 37	5 x 9
128 – 112	6 x 5
27 + 37	6 x 7
27 + 27	6 x 8

MIND-BENDER MATH

10 minutes

MATH CODES

Activity
64

Directions

Solve each math problem below and use the numbers given for each letter to discover the secret words.

a	b	c	d	e	f	g	h	i	j	k	l	m
10	20	30	40	50	5	6	8	7	9	14	15	16
n	o	p	q	r	s	t	u	v	w	x	y	z
18	12	21	22	25	28	35	60	70	100	3	44	48

MIND-BENDER MATH

1. _____ _____ _____ _____ _____
   10x3   3x5   4x3   3x10   7x2

2. _____ _____ _____ _____ _____
   7x4   7x5   3x4   10x7   10x5

3. _____ _____ _____ _____ _____
   20+10 6+2   5+5   4+3   20+5

4. _____ _____ _____ _____ _____ _____
   16–2   60–10 40–5   40–5   20–5   60–10

5. _____ _____ _____ _____ _____
   3+2   20+5   30+30 4+3   30+5

6. _____ _____ _____ _____ _____ _____
   6x5   4x2   10x5   2x25   7x4   10x5

7. _____ _____ _____ _____ _____ _____
   4x2   10x5   5x2   7x5   10x5   5x5

8. _____ _____ _____ _____ _____
   7x5   5x2   5x4   5x3   10x5

10
minutes

QUESTION AND ANSWER

Activity 65

Directions

Solve each multiplication problem. Use each answer's letter to discover a secret question and its answer.

MIND-BENDER MATH

1. 14 x 2 = W	**4.** 331 x 2 = I	**7.** 4,244 x 2 = T	**10.** 321 x 3 = N	**13.** 212 x 4 = L
2. 3,412 x 2 = M	**5.** 313 x 3 = A	**8.** 441 x 2 = H	**11.** 3,142 x 2 = P	**14.** 2,211 x 4 = ?
3. 324 x 2 = U	**6.** 2,332 x 3 = C	**9.** 1,322 x 30 = !	**12.** 1,241 x 2 = Y	**15.** 4,123 x 2 = O

____ ____ ____   ____ ____ ____
28   882   8,246   6,996 939   963

____ ____ ____ ____ ____ ____ ____ ____ ____
6,824 648   848 8,488 662 6,284 848 2,482 8,844

____   ____ ____ ____ ____
662   6,996 939   963   3,966

15 minutes

MATH TRIVIA

Directions

Solve each math trivia question below.

1. How many minutes in 2 hours? _____

2. How many dimes are in a dollar? _____

3. What is a 3-sided figure called? _____

4. Two tons is equal to how many pounds? _____

5. What mark separates the hour and the minutes when one is writing down time? _____

6. How many items in a dozen? _____

7. How many sides does a hexagon have? _____

8. What do you call the result of adding two numbers? _____

9. How many centimeters are in a meter? _____

10. How many months are in half of a year? _____

11. Which plane figure has 8 sides? _____

12. How many sides are there on a die? _____

13. How many years are in a decade? _____

14. How many hours are in a day? _____

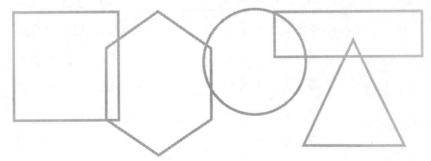

DIVISION FUN

Activity
67

Directions

Solve each division problem. Write each quotient as a number word in the number puzzle. See #3 Across. It has been done for you.

Across

3. $14 \div 2 = $ ___7___

5. $49 \div 7 = $ _____

8. $48 \div 6 = $ _____

9. $75 \div 5 = $ _____

11. $10 \div 10 = $ _____

12. $36 \div 9 = $ _____

14. $96 \div 8 = $ _____

16. $39 \div 3 = $ _____

18. $16 \div 4 = $ _____

Down

1. $78 \div 6 = $ _____

2. $35 \div 7 = $ _____

4. $22 \div 2 = $ _____

6. $81 \div 9 = $ _____

7. $27 \div 9 = $ _____

9. $56 \div 4 = $ _____

10. $30 \div 3 = $ _____

13. $0 \div 15 = $ _____

15. $18 \div 3 = $ _____

16. $14 \div 7 = $ _____

17. $50 \div 5 = $ _____

15 minutes

MIND-BENDER MATH

MONEY EQUATIONS

Activity
68

Directions

Solve each money trivia equation by writing and
solving a new number sentence.

1. number of nickels in a quarter + number of pennies in 6¢

   _____

2. number of dimes in $1 – number of quarters in $1

   _____

3. number of pennies in 25¢ ÷ number of nickels in 5¢

   _____

4. number of half-dollars in 50¢ x number of dimes in 50¢

   _____

5. number of quarters in 75¢ x number of quarters in $1

   _____

6. number of nickels in 30¢ – number of dimes in 30¢

   _____

7. number of pennies in 10¢ – number of pennies in one dime

   _____

8. number of quarters in 25¢ + number of nickels in 25¢

   _____

9. number of dimes in 90¢ ÷ number of nickels in 15¢

   _____

10. number of silver dollars in $1 x number of pennies in $1

   _____

MIND-BENDER MATH

10
minutes

AMAZING EQUATIONS

Activity 69

Directions

Follow the instructions below to work out this remarkable math equation. Be sure to complete the instructions in order. You will need a piece of scratch paper in order to solve some equations.

1. Write down the number of the month you were born. _____ (For instance, if you were born in April, write down 4).

2. Multiply the number above by 4.

_____ x 4 = _____

3. Add 13 to the number above.

_____ + 13 = _____

4. Multiply the number above by 25.

_____ x 25 = _____

5. Subtract 200 from the number above.

_____ − 200 = _____

6. Add the day of the month on which you were born to the number above.

_____ + _____ = _____

7. Multiply the number above by 2.

_____ x 2 = _____

8. Subtract 40 from the number above.

_____ − 40 = _____

9. Multiply the number above by 50.

_____ x 50 = _____

10. Add the last two digits of the year of your birth to the number above.

_____ + _____ = _____

11. Subtract 10,500 from the number above.

_____ − 10,500 = _____

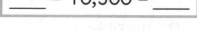

10 minutes

What's amazing about your answer? _____

MIXED PRACTICE

Activity
70

Directions

Solve each multiplication and division problem and complete the number puzzle.

MIND-BENDER MATH

Across

1. 3,608 ÷ 2 = _____

3. 52,160 ÷ 10 = _____

6. 485 x 8 = _____

8. 4,555 x 5 = _____

10. 784 ÷ 8 = _____

11. 4,013 x 2 = _____

12. 196 x 6 = _____

14. 1,792 x 2 = _____

17. 10,096 ÷ 4 = _____

Down

1. 7,725 ÷ 5 = _____

2. 387 ÷ 9 = _____

4. 295 x 9 = _____

5. 6,809 ÷ 1 = _____

7. 812 x 10 = _____

8. 6,717 x 4 = _____

9. 2,438 x 3 = _____

13. 183 ÷ 3 = _____

14. 562 x 7 = _____

15. 264 ÷ 6 = _____

16. 434 ÷ 7 = _____

15
minutes

NAME _____ DATE _____

CLEVER CODES

Activity 71

Directions

Study the codes carefully, and then decode the words. Each is the name of something you can eat. The first one has been started for you.

c	e	m
b	a	t
u	k	r

```
      l
  s       d
      j
```

1. ⌐ ⊔ □ ⊏   ___me_____

2. ┘ □ ⊓ ⊔   _____

3. ⊐ ┐ ⊏ ⊏ ⊔ ┌   _____

4. ⊐ ┌ ⊔ □ > <   _____

5. ∧ □ └   _____

6. < □ ∨ ⊏   _____

5 minutes

BEYOND BRAINY

WHAT'S MISSING?

Activity
72

Directions

Look carefully at the two pictures. There are five lines missing from the second picture. Draw in the missing lines.

BEYOND BRAINY

5
minutes

SHADOW PAIRS

Directions

Match the shadow parts that belong together.

Activity

BEYOND BRAINY

1.

a.

2.

b.

3.

c.

4.

d.

5.

e.

5 minutes

DOMINOES

Directions

Dominoes were used to create the puzzle below. The dominoes are placed vertically and horizontally in the puzzle. Circle each pair of numbers to match the domino used. Each domino was used one time.

Dominoes Used

| 1 1 | 1 2 | 4 4 | 4 5 |
| 5 1 | 5 2 | 5 3 | 5 5 |

BEYOND BRAINY

10 minutes

HIDDEN ANIMALS

Activity
75

Directions

Hidden inside each sentence are two or three animal names. Can you find them? Circle them and write them on the lines.

Example: Hel p ig loos! ➔ pig

1. Wash or sell the new costume.

   _____

2. Catherine uses nails to add.

   _____

3. The crowded room was packed with ogres!

   _____

4. Steffi Shalder came late to the party.

   _____

5. Charlotte requested a crown to cover her hairdo goof.

   _____

6. Mr. Roy Stern made Ernie stay after school.

   _____

BEYOND BRAINY

10
minutes

BEGIN AND END

Directions

Each phrase below is a clue for an answer that begins and ends with the same letter.

1. child's sidewalk game _____

2. a continent _____

3. songs sung alone _____

4. our national bird _____

5. a type of boat _____

6. long body of moving water _____

7. one of the sense organs _____

8. a common man's name _____

9. to quiet down _____

10. blue-green color _____

11. a young bird's noise _____

12. midday _____

13. the hardest mineral _____

14. the day before today _____

10
minutes

FRUIT EATERS

Directions

Read the clues in the box, and then answer the questions below.

> Only Paul and Tuki eat bananas.
>
> Only Tuki and Joanne eat grapes.
>
> Only Paul and Joanne eat apples.

BEYOND BRAINY

1. Who eats both bananas and grapes? _____

2. Who eats both grapes and apples? _____

3. Who eats apples but not grapes? _____

4. What does Joanne eat that Tuki doesn't? _____

5. What does Paul eat that Tuki doesn't? _____

5
minutes

DOUBLE LETTERS IN SPORTS

Activity
78

Directions

Answer each sports clue with a word that contains double letters. The first one has been done for you.

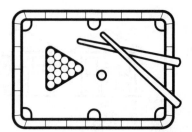

1. _____Pool_____ is a game played on a table with balls and cue sticks.

2. Basketball players try to throw a ball through a _____.

3. "Swing, _____!" is a cry heard at baseball games.

4. Bicyclists need two _____ on their bikes.

5. When playing _____ , your hands can't touch the ball.

6. Baseball players keep their eyes on the _____.

7. Kayakers need a _____ to move across the water.

8. In _____ , two players hit a ball across a net.

9. The only equipment _____ need is a pair of shoes.

10. _____ is a sport that requires snow.

BEYOND BRAINY

10 minutes

WHICH ONE'S DIFFERENT?

Directions

Study each row of pictures. Circle the one that is different from the others in that row.

1.

2.

3.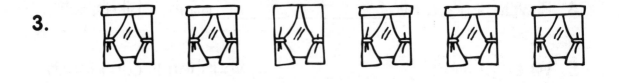

4.

5.

BEYOND BRAINY

5
minutes

DECODING

Activity

80

Directions

Match each number to the letter in the code to find the career names.

A	B	C	D	E	F	G	H	I	J	K	L	M
1	2	3	4	5	6	7	8	9	10	11	12	13

N	O	P	Q	R	S	T	U	V	W	X	Y	Z
14	15	16	17	18	19	20	21	22	23	24	25	26

1. 6 1 18 13 5 18 _____

2. 2 1 14 11 5 18 _____

3. 12 1 23 25 5 18 _____

4. 20 5 1 3 8 5 18 _____

5. 4 15 3 20 15 18 _____

6. 23 18 9 20 5 18 _____

7. 19 5 3 18 5 20 1 18 25 _____

8. 4 5 20 5 3 20 9 22 5 _____

9. 12 9 2 18 1 18 9 1 14 _____

10. 19 3 9 5 14 20 9 19 20 _____

11. 13 21 19 9 3 9 1 14 _____

12. 1 3 20 15 18 _____

13. 5 4 9 20 15 18 _____

14. 3 15 15 11 _____

15. 6 9 18 5 6 9 7 8 20 5 18 _____

10 minutes

MEMORY TEST

**Activity
81**

Directions

Look closely at the ten pictures. Give yourself
two minutes to look, then cover them up
and write down all those you can remember.

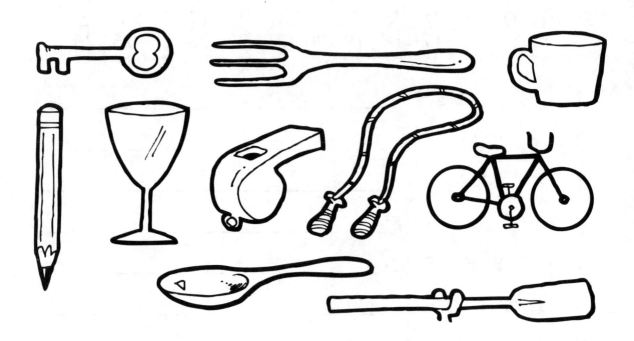

BEYOND BRAINY

1. _____   6. _____

2. _____   7. _____

3. _____   8. _____

4. _____   9. _____

5. _____   10. _____

**5
minutes**

EXPLAIN THE ERROR

Activity

82

Directions

Look closely at each picture below. Draw a circle around the mistake in each one. Then explain why the pictures are wrong.

1.  _____

_____

2.  _____

_____

3.  _____

_____

BEYOND BRAINY

5 minutes

FOLLOWING INSTRUCTIONS

Activity

83

Directions

Look at the shapes and letters in the box. Then follow the instructions to write the correct letters in the boxes below to discover the hidden message.

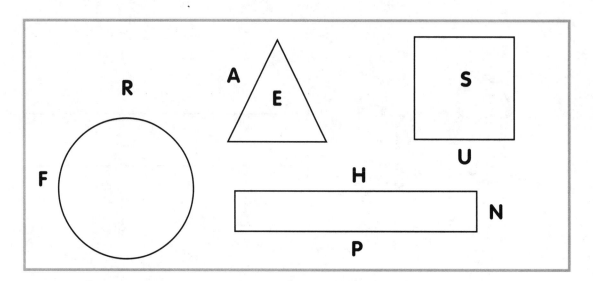

Write the letter to the right of the rectangle in box 12.

Write the letter to the left of the triangle in boxes 3 and 7.

Write the letter under the rectangle in box 4.

Write the letter above the rectangle in box 2.

Write the letter inside the triangle in boxes 5 and 9.

Write the letter under the square in box 11.

Write the letter inside the square in boxes 1 and 6.

Write the letter above the circle in box 8.

Write the letter to the left of the circle in box 10.

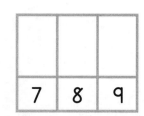

1	2	3	4	5	6

7	8	9

10	11	12

Famous Pairs

Activity
84

Directions

Use the words in the box to complete the famous pairs below. Then find the words in the word search.

FORK	NEW	PEPPER	WATER	BALL
DAY	OLD	SHOUT	SOUND	BAD
CENTS	WRITE	TOMATO	THEN	CATS

Beyond Brainy

```
G  A  E  L  O  T  T  R  H  I  K  V
H  X  H  R  J  U  E  U  I  W  O  J
M  Y  O  S  M  P  W  Y  O  A  G  G
R  Z  O  E  P  G  R  L  S  H  W  X
Z  L  V  E  T  F  I  P  W  A  S  N
D  L  P  O  E  H  T  S  T  E  K  J
T  O  M  A  T  O  E  E  O  L  N  S
S  T  N  E  C  B  R  N  L  U  I  B
T  Y  A  D  H  A  K  A  Y  J  N  B
A  F  O  R  K  D  B  K  L  S  S  D
C  N  E  O  H  Q  H  Z  U  B  T  V
B  B  L  T  L  T  Z  S  I  C  D  S
```

DOGS and _____

TWIST and _____

OLD and _____

NOW and _____

READ and _____

GOOD and _____

SAFE and _____

YOUNG and _____

KNIFE and _____

LETTUCE and _____

BAT and _____

NIGHT and _____

DOLLARS and _____

SOAP and _____

SALT and _____

10 minutes

Y IS A CONSONANT

Activity 85

Directions

Y is a vowel most of the time. It is a consonant just when it is the first letter of a word or a new syllable. Read each word. Follow the path of the words in which Y is a consonant (such as *yours*).

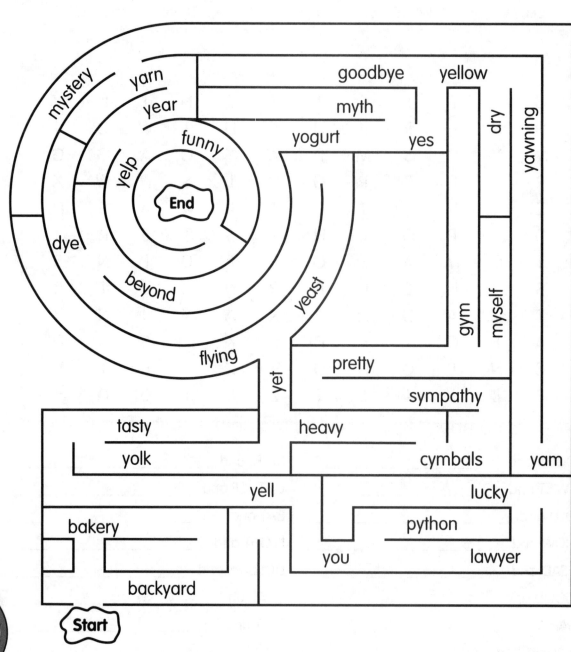

5 minutes

BEYOND BRAINY

PHONE CODES

Directions

Use the letters on the phone keypad to help you solve the phone code puzzles below.

1. Phil's phone number is **766-7837**. If someone asks for his number, Phil gives the name of an animal instead of telling the digits. Which animal does he name?

   ___ ___ ___ ___ ___ ___ ___

2. Henry's phone number is **626-4637**. If someone asks for his number, Henry gives the name of a fruit instead of telling the digits. Which fruit does he name?

   ___ ___ ___ ___ ___ ___ ___

3. Edna's phone number is **347-4464**. If someone asks for her number, Edna gives the name of a sport instead of telling the digits. Which sport does she name?

   ___ ___ ___ ___ ___ ___ ___

Beyond Brainy

10 minutes

WORD CHAIN

BEYOND BRAINY

Directions

Use the clues to help you fill in the blanks and circles. Only the circled letters change from one word to the next. The first two have been done for you.

1. bright-yellow precious metal   (g)   o   l   d

2. without fear   (b)   o   l   d

3. a metal fastening for a door

4. a young horse

5. shed the skin, hair, or shell

6. a small underground animal

7. an open place

8. grasp and keep

9. a fungus

10. calm, warm, gentle

11. not tamed

12. to wither

13. the desire to do something

14. side of a room

15. a round, bouncing toy

16. speak or say in a loud voice

17. trip

18. to load with room for nothing more

19. drawer for keeping papers in order

20. heap up or stack

15 minutes

NAME _____   DATE _____

BIRTHDAYS

Directions

Eight children, including Sarah, will all turn ten years of age this year. From the clues given, determine the month of each child's birth. Mark an **X** in each correct box.

Clues:

- A common holiday is celebrated on Jill's birthday.
- Andrea's birthday is before Jeff's but after Millie's and Sarah's.
- Sarah's birthday is exactly one month after Millie's.
- Andrew's birthday is during the winter months.
- Max's birthday comes after Andrea's but before Jeff's.

BEYOND BRAINY

	Feb. 15	Mar. 24	April 1	May 1	July 10	Sept. 9	Oct. 15	Dec. 25
Andrea								
Andrew								
Sarah								
Sam								
Jill								
Jeff								
Millie								
Max								

10 minutes

HIDDEN MEANINGS

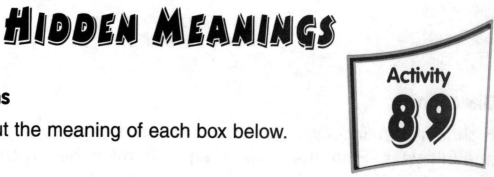

Activity 89

Directions

Figure out the meaning of each box below.

<u>Stand</u> I	cycle cycle cycle	T O U C H

1. _____ 4. _____ 7. _____

	NOON GOOD	Jack

2. _____ 5. _____ 8. _____

	chair	TI*JUST*ME

3. _____ 6. _____ 9. _____

BEYOND BRAINY

10 minutes

LIVING THINGS

Activity
90

Directions

Find the names of the living things in the grid.
Write them under the correct headings below.

c	r	o	c	o	d	i	l	e
b	k	p	e	n	g	u	i	n
e	o	s	p	a	r	r	o	w
e	a	l	i	z	a	r	d	x
t	l	w	a	s	p	o	w	l
l	a	b	e	e	l	i	o	n
e	k	a	n	g	a	r	o	o
a	l	l	i	g	a	t	o	r

Mammals

1. _____

2. _____

3. _____

Birds

1. _____

2. _____

3. _____

Reptiles

1. _____

2. _____

3. _____

Insects

1. _____

2. _____

3. _____

10
minutes

93 #2938 101 Activities for Fast Finishers

A TO Z

Activity 91

Directions

Make a list of five-letter words. One letter in each word has been placed for you. How many can you make?

BEYOND BRAINY

a

b

c

d

e

f

g

h

i

j

k

l

m

n

o

p

q

r

s

t

u

v

w

x

y

z

15 minutes

CRAYON SUDOKU

Activity
92

Directions

Fill every square with an indicated color. No color can be repeated in a column, row, or box.

R = Red	**Y** = Yellow	**B** = Blue
O = Orange	**G** = Green	**P** = Purple

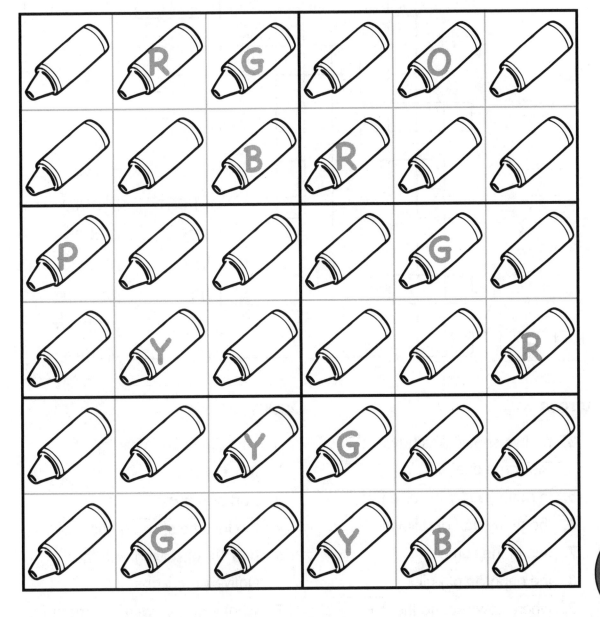

Beyond Brainy

15 minutes

STARTS WITH "P"

Activity
93

Directions

Use the words in the box and the clues to help fill in the puzzle with words that start with the letter "p."

BEYOND BRAINY

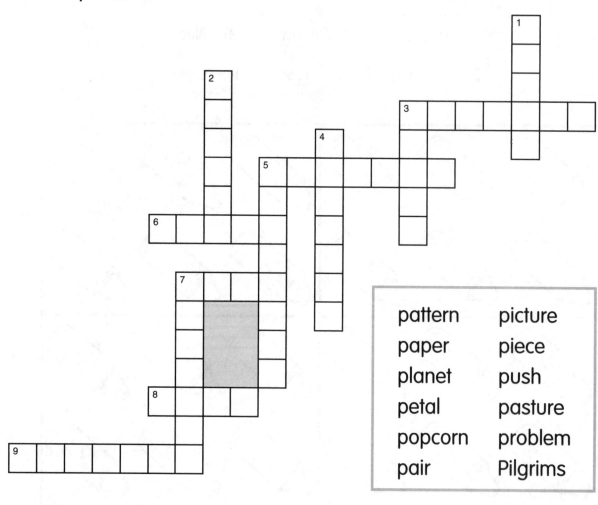

pattern	picture
paper	piece
planet	push
petal	pasture
popcorn	problem
pair	Pilgrims

Across

3. no two snowflakes have the same one
5. in math you try to solve this
6. the pretty part of a flower
7. two of the same
8. the opposite of pull
9. where cows spend the day

Down

1. something you write on
2. Mars is one
3. part of a pizza
4. the favorite snack at the movies
5. had Thanksgiving with the Native Americans
7. what you take with a camera

10 minutes

ANALOGIES

Directions

Analogies are comparisons. Complete each analogy below. An example has been done for you.

Nephew is to uncle as niece is to aunt.

1. _____ is to wings as fish is to fins.

2. Tennis is to _____ as baseball is to bat.

3. Author is to story as poet is to _____ .

4. Wide is to narrow as _____ is to short.

5. Dirt is to forest as _____ is to desert.

6. Frame is to picture as curtain is to _____ .

7. Sing is to song as _____ is to book.

8. Braces are to _____ as contact lenses are to eyes.

9. _____ is to flake as rain is to drop.

10. Scissors are to _____ as pen is to write.

11. Hat is to head as _____ is to foot.

12. Hammer is to nail as screwdriver is to _____ .

13. Fingers are to _____ as toes are to feet.

14. _____ is to pig as neigh is to horse.

15. Second is to _____ as day is to week.

BEYOND BRAINY

10 minutes

HOW OLD?

Directions

Use the information given to help you figure out how old these kids are. Circle your final answers.

BEYOND BRAINY

1. Jim's little sister is four. In two years, Jim will be twice as old as she is now. How old is Jim now?

3. Ben is six years older than his brother. The sum of their ages is the same as three times the younger brother's age. How old are Ben and his brother?

2. Kate's sister is fifteen. In four years, Kate will be one year younger than her sister is now. How old is Kate?

4. Ana is four years older than her little brother. In two years, Ana will be twice as old as her brother is now. How old are Ana and her brother now.

10 minutes

Mystery Money

Activity
96

Directions

Read the problems below and write down the bills and coins used to make the designated amount.

Hint: $2-bills are allowed.

1. 1 bill and 5 coins equal $2.51

_____

_____

2. 2 bills and 6 coins equal $10.18

_____

_____

3. 3 bills and 7 coins equal $3.15

_____

_____

4. 5 bills and 9 coins equal $90.99

_____

_____

5. 4 bills and 6 coins equal $19.64

_____

_____

6. 5 bills and 2 coins equal $24.35

_____

_____

BEYOND BRAINY

15 minutes

FINDING HOME

Activity

97

Directions

You are lost. Can you find your home by following the directions below? Color each of the houses you touch red. Color your home a different color.

1. Begin in the most northwest home.
2. Move three houses east.
3. Move one house south.
4. Move two houses southwest.
5. Move one house west.
6. Move three houses northeast.
7. Move two houses southeast.
8. Move five houses west.
9. Move two houses north.
10. Move three houses southeast. This is your home.

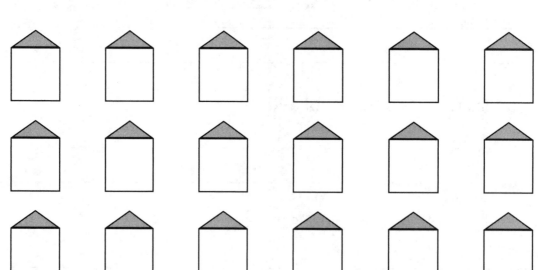

5 minutes

BEYOND BRAINY

NAME _____   DATE _____

HIDDEN PRIZE

Directions

Find the points on the graph that are indicated below.
Each point will give you a letter of the hidden prize.
Can you discover the secret?

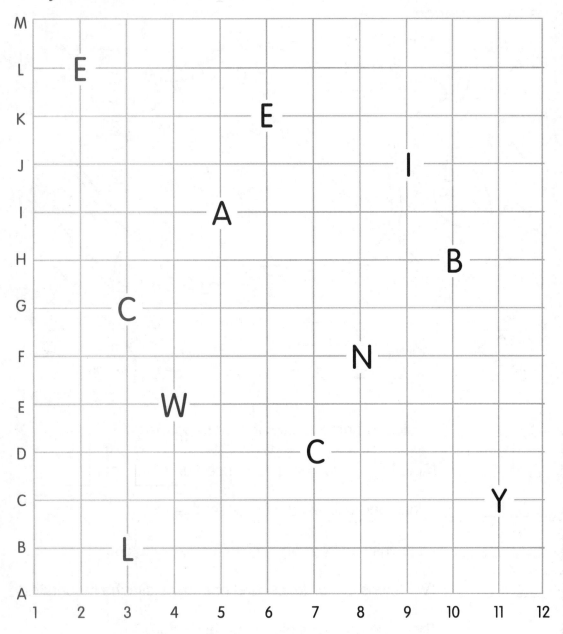

Jim won:

___   ___ ___ ___   ___ ___ ___ ___ ___ ___ ___
5,I   8,F 2,L 4,E   10,H 9,J 3,G 11,C 7,D 3,B 6,K

MAP TRUE OR FALSE

Activity

99

Directions

Look at the map and the symbols on the map key below. Then read the sentences that follow and answer true or false. If it is false, write the correct answer above the sentence.

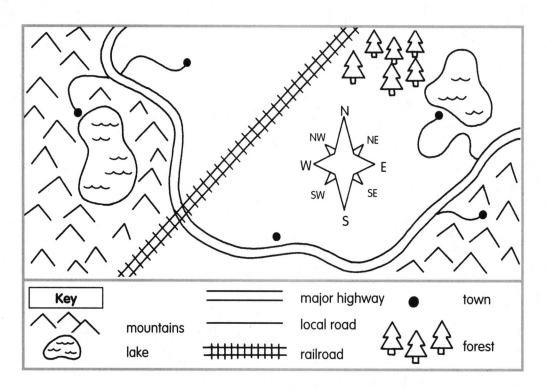

Key
mountains   —————— major highway   ●   town
lake   ———— local road
    ┼┼┼┼┼┼┼┼ railroad   forest

1. _____ A railroad track runs southwest to northeast.

2. _____ Mountains cover the northern section of the map.

3. _____ A lake and a forest are in the southeast.

4. _____ All towns can be reached by the major highway.

5. _____ Two towns are by lakes, and one town is in the mountains.

6. _____ There are no towns along the railroad track.

7. _____ There is a large forest east of the lake and west of the railroad.

8. _____ The southernmost town is next to the major highway.

10 minutes

BEYOND BRAINY

ODD ONE OUT

Activity 100

Directions

One word in each group below is in a different category than the others. Find that word and circle it in the puzzle.

```
R   E   R   H   O   T   D   O   G   S   G   S
A   T   J   A   T   I   Z   R   J   A   H   R
C   W   I   K   A   U   E   X   B   O   A   R
C   H   H   U   P   R   Z   H   V   B   P   E
O   G   N   I   X   F   T   E   Y   J   J   T
O   T   I   V   S   E   L   D   F   X   T   T
N   R   C   P   L   P   N   H   S   G   A   U
I   S   E   L   V   A   E   B   U   J   H   B
F   R   A   S   C   R   K   R   S   Y   R   C
R   W   O   G   A   G   O   T   A   M   O   T
V   G   V   X   X   R   G   O   N   H   F   I
S   F   P   T   G   R   E   Y   N   X   K   R
```

BEYOND BRAINY

RELISH, HOT DOG, MUSTARD, KETCHUP	FORK, SPOON, SHOVEL, KNIFE
CATHY, CAROL, SUSAN, CHERYL	CARNATION, ROSE, DAISY, TOMATO
PIE, CAKE, BROWNIE, CANDY BAR	BOY, LAD, AUNT, MAN
SPINACH, CELERY, BROCCOLI, GRAPEFRUIT	LAUGH, CRY, CHUCKLE, GIGGLE
DUCK, TURKEY, GOOSE, PIG	SHOUT, WHISPER, SCREAM, YELL
MARKER, ERASER, CHALK, PEN	DOG, GOLDFISH, PARAKEET, RACCOON
BAGEL, MUFFIN, BREAD, BUTTER	HAT, GLOVES, WALLET, BELT

10 minutes

RIDDLES

Activity
101

Directions

Use the words and phrases in the box to answer the riddles below. Then complete the puzzle.

BEYOND BRAINY

Tell it a yolk.
nine
a conversation
a newspaper
a bed
silence
a ton
the sidewalk
address
a chair
They all do.

Across

2. What has a head and a foot but no body?
4. How do you make an egg laugh?
5. What clothes does a house wear?
7. What's the hardest part about learning to skate?
8. Forward I am heavy, but backward I am "not." What am I?
9. What is black and white and read all over?
10. What takes two people to hold up but cannot be lifted?

Down

1. Some months have 30 days, some months have 31 days. How many have 28?
3. If two's company and three's a crowd, what are a four and five?
5. What has four legs, a back, but no body?
6. This is no sooner spoken than broken. What is it?

10
minutes

ANSWER KEY

Activity 1
Answers will vary.

Activity 2
horse—saddle
scales—fish
down—duck
paper—pen
camel—hump
bottle—glass
silk—worm
kidney—heart

Activity 3
Answers will vary.

Activity 4
1. bed   6. beak
2. bee   7. below
3. bell   8. berry
4. beard   9. bean
5. bear   10. begin

Activity 5
1. soft, duck
2. hand, gold
3. rich, long
4. coat, song
5. draw, read
6. moon, foot
7. stop, wool
8. west, wing
9. ball, feet
10. sock, bell

Activity 6
1. raincoat
2. moonlight
3. lifeboat
4. notebook
5. crossroad
6. toothbrush
7. photograph
8. classroom
9. spaceship
10. honeycomb

Activity 7
Possible answers:
through, thread, throat, thrifty,
enough, enemy, although,
spread, sprain, spring, bough,
bead, boat, nifty, rough, read,
rain, ring

Activity 8
1. zebra
2. lion
3. giraffe
4. camel
5. monkey (or donkey)
6. tortoise
7. elephant
8. raccoon
9. gorilla
10. horse
11. horse
12. zebra, lion, giraffe,
    camel, monkey (or
    donkey), tortoise,
    raccoon
13. elephant, gorilla

Activity 9
1. balloon   10. finger
2. sparrow   11. pony
3. football   12. doctor
4. winter   13. jungle
5. yellow   14. chair
6. strawberry   15. birthday
7. flour   16. people
8. money   17. elephant
9. cheese   18. stable or
                    tables

Activity 10
1. sauce
2. groom
3. chips
4. ball
5. jam
6. pepper
7. fork
8. downs

Activity 11
Possible answers:
Brigit, bell, bat, bush, berries,
bucket, bottle, backpack, box,
bike, balloon, boy, bread,
basket, bee, bird, brick,
branches, bark, buttons,
blade (of knife)

Activity 12
1. k   5. l
2. g   6. w
3. b   7. w
4. t   8. s
9.–12. Answers will vary.

Activity 13
1. flamingo
2. school
3. tennis
4. question
5. tractor
6. octagon
7. newspaper
8. mountain
9. penguin
10. lizard
11. lettuce
12. library

Activity 14
Answers will vary.

Activity 15
1. Row 5
2. Rows 1 and 2
3. Row 3
4. Row 4
5. Row 6
6. tops, spot, pots, stop,
   post (or opts)

ANSWER KEY (cont.)

Activity 16
1. sick
2. lion
3. snake
4. four
5. pony
6. first
7. city
8. dry
9. pink
10. duck
11. shoes
12. mouse

Activity 17
able—capable—competent
alarm—frighten—terrify
big—huge—large
danger—peril—hazard
divide—separate—split
hurt—injure—wound
interrogate—question—ask
mistake—error—blunder
world—globe—Earth

Activity 18
1. hamburger
2. peach
3. banana
4. avocado
5. cheese
6. cucumber
7. lemon
8. apricot

a. apricot
b. avocado
c. banana
d. cheese
e. cucumber
f. hamburger
g. lemon
h. peach

Activity 19
1. tale
2. hare
3. fare
4. scent
5. buy
6. lone
7. too
8. aide
9. beach
10. pair
11. great
12. alter
13. air
14. mourning
15. isle

Activity 20
1. platypus
2. hedgehog
3. penguin
4. monkey
5. sparrow
6. alligator
7. zebra
8. opossum
9. rabbit
10. stork
11. parrot
12. pelican
13. octopus
14. panther

Activity 21
Long E: treat, bead, scream, repeat, seats, steal, leaf, reading, speak
Long A: steak, great, break
Short E: heavy, measure, death, deaf, bread, wealth, meant, weather, ahead, already, breath, instead

Activity 22
1. t
2. r
3. u
4. e
5. w
6. m

Activity 23
Colors: beige, purple, violet, yellow
Birds: ostrich, penguin, sparrow, swallow
Vegetables: cabbage, lettuce, turnip, squash
Reptiles: gecko, crocodile, lizard, snake

Activity 24
1. geese
2. mice
3. feet
4. men
5. people
6. children
7. women
8. axes

Activity 25
1. horse
2. crocodile, alligator
3. car
4. fly, mosquito
5. farm
6. tiger
7. Christmas tree
8. milk
9. trash truck
10. piano
11. star
12. couch, sofa

Activity 26
1. shouted, yelled, whispered
2. screaming
3. shouted, hissed, yelled
4. said
5. tell
6. barking
7. shouted, hissed, yelled
8. shouted, hissed, yelled, whispered
9. talk
10. hooted

Activity 27
1. beast, belt
2. march, lump
3. thief, smoke, ship

Activity 28
Possible answers:
1. 2, 1, 5, 4, 3
2. 1, 3, 5, 2, 4
3. 4, 2, 1, 5, 3
4. 1, 3, 4, 2, 5
5. 4, 3, 2, 1, 5
6. 3, 5, 1, 2, 4

ANSWER KEY (cont.)

Activity 29
1. Tracy packed her coat.
2. Tracy packed her socks.
3. Tracy packed her pajamas.
4. Tracy packed her journal.
5. Tracy fell asleep.

Activity 30
1. Let, !
2. They, .
3. Why, ?
4. She, .
5. Get, !
6. Stop, .
7. Did, ?
8. Please, .
9. Were, ?
10. Wow, !
11. Those, .
12. Look, !
13. Clean, .
14. How, ?
15. What, ?

Activity 31

Activity 32
1. softer
2. taller
3. warmest
4. fastest
5. messiest
6. heavier
7. brightest
8. tinier
9. loudest
10. colder

Activity 33
1. Does your grandma have white hair?
2. Jacki found a wallet yesterday.
3. I just saw a shooting star.
4. Did you hide the money?
5. He won the race this afternoon.
6. Will you ask for a game?
7. Stop chasing the puppy.
8. Did Victoria find my missing homework?
9. My refrigerator has stopped working.
10. Logan quickly crossed over the bridge.

Activity 34
1. hen pen
2. far star
3. hot pot
4. hare chair
5. ship trip
6. loose goose
7. best rest
8. mad dad
9. big wig
10. book nook
11. slow crow
12. lunch bunch
13. wet jet
14. nice mice
15. cat hat

Activity 35
1. listening carefully
2. slow down
3. getting angry
4. teasing
5. remind you of something
6. ready to go
7. needs to hurry
8. getting into trouble
9. acting or looking the same
10. in good shape

Activity 36
1. 7, 8
2. 5, 7
3. 8, 16
4. 7, 11
5. 9, 11
6. 10, 11
7. 7, 9
8. 10, 20

Activity 37
9, 3, 6, and 7
8, 4, 6, and 7
3, 4, 8, and 10

Activity 38

Activity 39

Activity 40
Clockwise from top:
1. 4, 3
2. 1, 3, 2, 6
3. 7, 9, 12, 11
4. 1, 5, sum = 11
5. 2, 4, 5
6. 4, 2, 8, sum = 20

ANSWER KEY (cont.)

Activity 41
1. 563
2. 39
3. 92
4. 291
5. 563
6. 563, 365
7. 563, 481, 365, 291, 123, 92, 39

Activity 42
55 squares

Activity 43
1.

3	2	5	1	4
1	23	2	23	3
2	5	3	4	1
4	27	4	24	5
5	3	1	4	2

2.

5	4	3	1	2
4	33	5	21	3
3	5	4	2	1
1	21	2	24	5
2	3	1	5	4

Activity 44
1. 341;
   three hundred forty-one
2. 254;
   two hundred fifty-four
3. 165,
   one hundred sixty-five
4. 523;
   five hundred twenty-three
5. 436;
   four hundred thirty-six
6. 312;
   three hundred twelve
7. 654;
   six hundred fifty-four
8. 125;
   one hundred twenty-five

Activity 45
1.

+	4	=		
3		1	−	5
=	7			=
	−			2
	4	=	3	+

Start →

2.

−	9	=	9	=
8		7		5
=		+		+
1		2 ↑		4

Start

Activity 46
1. 6, 10, 20, 30, 25, 40
2. 5, 15, 30, 50, 80, 100
3. 16, 36, 31, 62, 70, 140

Activity 47
1. 9
2. 4
3. 17
4. 18
5. 24

Activity 48
1. 6
2. 48
3. 14
4. 21
5. 6
6. 32

Activity 49
1. 20 and 17
2. 13 and 12
3. 12
4. 13

Activity 50
1. $40.55
2. $18.01
3. $2.00
4. $80.00
5. $1.48
6. $12.09
7. $43.39
8. $6.20
9. $60.20
10. $7.12
11. $21.65
12. $47.44
13. $9.10
14. $10.20
Answer: growing on trees

Activity 51
1. bottom row: 7, 13, 14, 14, 17, 18, 21, 24, 24, 24, 23, 30, 33
   Rule: top row + middle row = bottom row
2. bottom row: 6, 8, 15, 18, 28, 20, 24, 25, 45, 14, 40, 100, 24
   Rule: top row x middle row = bottom row
3. bottom row: 5, 5, 7, 6, 10, 11, 5, 6, 9, 29, 6, 5, 80
   Rule: top row − middle row = bottom row

Activity 52
1. zebra
2. apple
3. broom
4. green
5. mouse
6. butter

Activity 53
1.
2.
3.
4.
5.

Activity 54
1. 9
3. 15
2. 24
4. 30
5. 27
6. 60

Activity 55
1. 40, 84, 16, 68, 24, 52
2. 26, 70, 2, 54, 10, 38
3. 49, 115, 13, 91, 25, 67
4. 10, 21, 4, 17, 6, 13
5. 26, 70, 2, 54, 10, 38

Activity 56
1. 3
2. 6
3. 9
4. 12
5. 15
6. 18
7. 21
8. 24
9. 27
10. 30
11. 33
12. 36
13. 4 and 8

Activity 57
Blue fish (even): 3 x 4, 8 + 8,
9 x 2, 6 x 2, 7 x 2, 8 + 10,
5 x 4, 7 + 5, 4 x 4, 12 x 2

Red fish (odd): 5 x 5, 3 x 5,
3 x 7, 7 x 5, 5 x 3, 12 + 7,
15 + 6, 3 x 3, 12 + 9, 7 x 3

Activity 58
1. 15
2. 10
3. 10
4. 19
5. 16
6. 20
7. 12
8. 15
9. 17
10. 14
11. 10
12. 165
13. 24
14. 9
15. 32
16. 50
17. 11, 13, 15, 17, 19
18. 109

Activity 59
24 = 8 x 3, 12 x 2, 4 x 6,
      3 x 8
12 = 2 x 6, 3 x 4
40 = 2 x 20, 10 x 4, 8 x 5
30 = 6 x 5, 3 x 10

Activity 60
1. pear
2. apple
3. peach
4. banana
5. orange
6. grape

Activity 61
Clockwise from number
provided:
1. 5, 6, 13, 8, 9, 10, 15, 7
2. 7, 12, 17, 97, 37, 15, 9,
   27
3. 9, 12, 18, 15, 30, 24, 21,
   27
4. 3, 4, 5, 7, 6, 10, 12, 8

Activity 62
1. 18
2. 12
3. 26
4. 35
5. 33
6. 13
7. 24
8. 25

Activity 63
21 − 15 = 2 x 3
4 + 5 = 3 x 3
36 − 24 = 3 x 4
13 + 8 = 3 x 7
38 − 11 = 3 x 9
9 + 15 = 4 x 6
45 − 13 = 4 x 8
3 + 12 = 5 x 3
17 + 18 = 5 x 7
22 + 23 = 5 x 9
46 − 16 = 6 x 5
19 + 23 = 6 x 7
60 − 12 = 6 x 8
13 + 15 = 7 x 4
12 + 37 = 7 x 7
33 + 30 = 7 x 9
77 − 37 = 8 x 5
128 − 112 = 8 x 2
27 + 37 = 8 x 8
27 + 27 = 9 x 6

Activity 64
1. clock
2. stove
3. chair
4. kettle
5. fruit
6. cheese
7. heater
8. table

Answer Key (cont.)

Activity 65

1. 28	9. 3,966
2. 6,824	10. 963
3. 648	11. 6,284
4. 662	12. 2,482
5. 939	13. 848
6. 6,996	14. 8,844
7. 8,488	15. 8,246
8. 882	

Answer: Who can multiply?
I can!

Activity 66

1. 120	8. sum
2. 10	9. 100
3. triangle	10. 6
4. 4,000	11. octagon
5. colon	12. 6
6. 12	13. 10
7. 6	14. 24

Activity 67

Across
3. 7
5. 7
8. 8
9. 15
11. 1
12. 4
14. 12
16. 13
18. 4

Down
1. 13
2. 5
4. 11
6. 9
7. 3
9. 14
10. 10
13. 0
15. 6
16. 2
17. 10

Activity 68

1. 5 + 6 = 11
2. 10 − 4 = 6
3. 25 ÷ 1 = 25
4. 1 x 5 = 5
5. 3 x 4 = 12
6. 6 − 3 = 3
7. 10 − 10 = 0
8. 1 + 5 = 6
9. 9 ÷ 3 = 3
10. 1 x 100 = 100

Activity 69

Check the page for accuracy.
Answer: Student should end
up with his or her birthday.

Activity 70

Across
1. 1,804
3. 5,216
6. 3,880
8. 22,775
10. 98
11. 8,026
12. 1,176
14. 3,584
17. 2,524

Down
1. 1,545
2. 43
4. 2,655
5. 6,809
7. 8,120
8. 26,868
9. 7,314
13. 61
14. 3,934
15. 44
16. 62

Activity 71

1. meat	4. bread
2. cake	5. jam
3. butter	6. salt

Activity 72

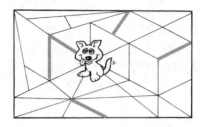

Activity 73

1. c	4. a
2. e	5. d
3. b	

Activity 74

Activity 75
1. horse, hen
2. cat, snail, toad
3. crow, wasp, hog
4. fish, camel
5. otter, crow, dog
6. oyster, deer

Activity 76
1. hopscotch
2. Antarctica; Europe; Asia;
   Africa; Australia
3. solos
4. eagle
5. kayak
6. river
7. eye
8. Bob; David (may vary)
9. hush
10. aqua
11. peep; tweet
12. noon
13. diamond
14. yesterday

Answer Key (cont.)

Activity 77
1. Tuki
2. Joanne
3. Paul
4. apples
5. apples

Activity 78
1. Pool
2. hoop
3. batter
4. wheels
5. soccer
6. ball
7. paddle
8. tennis
9. runners
10. Skiing

Activity 79
1. first house
2. sixth chair
3. third window
4. second dog
5. fifth lamp

Activity 80
1. farmer
2. banker
3. lawyer
4. teacher
5. doctor
6. writer
7. secretary
8. detective
9. librarian
10. scientist
11. musician
12. actor
13. editor
14. cook
15. firefighter

Activity 81
Check page for accuracy.

Activity 82
1. The TV is unplugged.
2. Elephants don't have horse tails.
3. There is no rain in outer space.

Activity 83
Hidden Message: Shapes are fun.

Activity 84
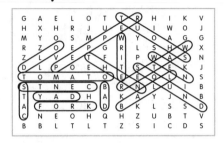

Activity 85
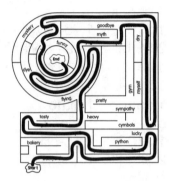

Activity 86
1. rooster
2. mangoes
3. fishing

Activity 87
1. gold
2. bold
3. bolt
4. colt
5. molt
6. mole
7. hole
8. hold
9. mold
10. mild
11. wild
12. wilt
13. will
14. wall
15. ball
16. call
17. fall
18. fill
19. file
20. pile

Activity 88
Andrea—July 10
Andrew—February 15
Sarah—May 1
Sam—March 24
Jill—December 25
Jeff—October 15
Millie—April 1
Max—September 9

Activity 89
1. I understand
2. holy cow
3. all over the place; all mixed up
4. tricycle
5. good afternoon
6. high chair
7. touchdown
8. jack in the box
9. just in time

Activity 90
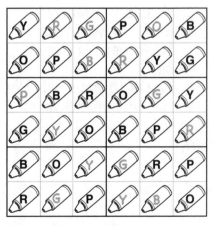

Mammals: kangaroo, koala, lion
Reptiles: alligator, crocodile, lizard
Birds: owl, penguin, sparrow
Insects: bee, beetle, wasp

Activity 91
Answers will vary.

Activity 92

ANSWER KEY (cont.)

Activity 93
Across
3. pattern
5. problem
6. petal
7. pair
8. push
9. pasture

Down
1. paper
2. planet
3. piece
4. popcorn
5. Pilgrims
7. picture

Activity 94
1. Bird
2. racket
3. poem
4. tall
5. sand
6. window
7. read
8. teeth
9. Snow
10. cut
11. shoe (or sock)
12. screw
13. hands
14. Oink
15. minute

Activity 95
1. Jim is 6 years old now.
2. Kate is 10 years old.
3. Ben is 12 years old. His little brother is 6 years old.
4. Ana is 10 years old. Her little brother is 6 years old.

Activity 96
1. 1 $2-bill, 1 quarter, 2 dimes, 1 nickel, 1 penny
2. 2 $5-bills, 3 nickels, 3 pennies
3. 3 $1-bills, 2 nickels, 5 pennies
4. 4 $20-bills, 1 $10-bill, 3 quarters, 2 dimes, 4 pennies
5. 1 $10-bill, 1 $5-bill, 2 $2-bills, 1 half-dollar coin, 1 dime, 4 pennies
6. 1 $20-bill, 4 $1-bills, 1 quarter, 1 dime
   or
   1 $10-bill, 2 $5-bills, 2 $2-bills, 1 quarter, 1 dime

Activity 97
Check page for accuracy.
Home = bottom row, fourth house from the left

Activity 98
Jim won: a new bicycle

Activity 99
1. true
2. false; western and southeastern
3. false; northeast
4. false; only one, other towns reached by local roads
5. true
6. true
7. false; west of lake, east of railroad
8. true

Activity 100

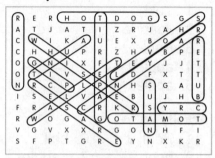

Circled words: hot dog, Susan, candy bar, grapefruit, pig, eraser, butter, shovel, tomato, aunt, cry, whisper, raccoon, wallet

Activity 101
Across
2. a bed
4. Tell it a yolk.
5. address
7. the sidewalk
8. a ton
9. a newspaper
10. a conversation

Down
1. They all do.
3. nine
5. a chair
6. silence